D1241457

THE NEED TO KNOW LIBRARY™

EVERYTHING YOU NEED TO KNOW ABOUT

CULTURAL APPROPRIATION

LISA A. CRAYTON

Rosen
YA™
New York

Published in 2019 by The Rosen Publishing Group, Inc.
29 East 21st Street, New York, NY 10010

First Edition

Library of Congress Cataloging-in-Publication Data

Names: Crayton, Lisa A., author.
Title: Everything you need to know about cultural appropriation / Lisa A. Crayton.
Description: New York : Rosen Publishing, 2019 | Series: The need to know library | Audience: Grades 7–12. | Includes bibliographical references and index.
Identifiers: LCCN 2017055274| ISBN 9781508179184 (library bound) | ISBN 9781508179276 (pbk.)
Subjects: LCSH: Multiculturalism—United States—Juvenile literature. | Cultural property—United States—Juvenile literature.
Classification: LCC HM1271 .C725 2018 | DDC 305.800973—dc23
LC record available at https://lccn.loc.gov/2017055274

Manufactured in the United States of America

On the cover: A festivalgoer wearing a Native American headdress poses at the June 2016 Parklife Festival. The festival features contemporary music artists and takes place in Manchester, England. It has no identifiable ties to any Native American culture.

CONTENTS

INTRODUCTION

"Sí, quiero arroz con pollo." ("Yes, I want chicken and rice.") Such a simple statement, but a huge accomplishment for Linda, who beamed while answering Mrs. Concepción's question. She loved Rosie's mom's cooking, especially the authentic Puerto Rican dish. Linda had practiced the phrase for weeks. By Mrs. Concepción's expression, she must have nailed it. It wasn't as easy as she had hoped, but she practiced a lot. Linda planned on taking a class the following year to improve her Spanish-language skills. The next day at school, Linda shared the story with her friends. They were all impressed, including her friend Terry.

With Halloween fast approaching, Terry had been looking for the perfect costume, and he thought his quest was finally over. He picked one designed to look like a Native American tribal leader. However, when he wore it to school, some people were outraged. Terry couldn't understand why some of their friends had applauded Linda's interest in Spanish, but criticized his costume choice. It's just a costume. What's the big deal?

The big deal? Linda's desire to speak Spanish celebrated a culture that wasn't her own, and it showed appreciation for that culture, including its cuisine. Conversely, Terry's costume choice was a form of cultural appropriation. Cultural appropriation is when someone adopts another culture's identifiable, tangible elements

Working together on projects of any kind with a diverse group is one way to appreciate and connect meaningfully with members of cultures different from your own.

without honoring their cultural significance. Cultural appropriation includes everything from clothing to hairstyles, jewelry, musical style, and even food. Linda's decision to learn Spanish showed a desire to learn more about another culture. Terry's decision ignored the cultural importance of Native American attire and how treating such attire as a costume could offend Native American people. Many have fallen into a similar trap. They either were unaware of cultural appropriation or felt their own enjoyment mattered more than respect for others' heritage. In either case, cultural appropriation is inexcusable.

Cultural appropriation happens all the time. However, there are certain times when it is more common. For example, every Halloween, the issue becomes a topic of discussion. So many inappropriate outfits are worn on Halloween without thought about how they may be offensive.

Many parents buy outfits for young kids, helping to spur culturally insensitive buying habits that continue throughout life. Some outfits, such as ones that mimic traditional Native American attire, have been popular for years, despite their insensitivity. Others crop up when new fads—often movies—spark interest in a certain culture. Whatever its origin, instances of cultural appropriation reinforce the need for everybody to understand the issue.

Nobody is exempt from the effects of cultural appropriation. Everybody knows or meets people who belong to victimized groups in their day-to-day lives, and these people are often hurt by actions that rob their culture of value and meaning. When everybody better understands cultural appropriation, can identify how and why it happens, and becomes actively involved in treating other cultures with respect, we are all better off.

Most people don't think they can have an impact on today's cultural climate. Yet everybody can have a positive impact and connect meaningfully with other cultures. The first step is understanding cultural appropriation. Next is choosing to be different by not engaging in problematic behavior. Finally, a deliberate effort to confront cultural appropriation can help educate others on how to engage meaningfully and respectfully with other cultures.

CHAPTER ONE

IDENTITY THEFT

Today, we live in a multicultural world where we regularly interact with different cultures in school, in our communities, and online. We regularly see, experience, and encounter situations where other cultural groups' identities and cultural expressions are thrust into our day.

Consider this imaginary—yet common—occurrence: a school costume party. At this event, students are adorned in many outfits that spark fun. Others are outfitted in costumes that raise questions and concerns:

- A white student wears fake Native American regalia, including an elaborate headdress.
- A light-skinned Latino student models his afro wig and wears blackface.
- Three Asian-American students sport Mexican clothing, speak in exaggerated accents, and pretend to be part of a Mariachi band.

All are excited about their outfits, believing they chose well. But did they? To classmates with heritage in the cultures depicted in these choices, the answer is a resounding no. In fact, affected students might see each costume as a prime example of cultural appropriation.

Cultural appropriation is a form of identity theft. It happens when someone adopts another culture's identifiable elements without honoring their cultural origin or significance. In this example, each costume reduces a specific culture to just an outfit or symbol, something to be put on for fun and games. Furthermore, it fails to acknowledge the very real discrimination or oppression members of such cultures live with—something they never have the option of simply "taking off." Culture is so much more than a costume.

CULTURE DEFINED

Culture is defined as behavior and elements shared by a group of people. It includes many things associated with that group, including people's beliefs, food, music, clothing, and religion. Culture and race are often interconnected.

We live in a multicultural world filled with opportunities to celebrate others' cultural backgrounds. On the positive side, we can interact with other cultures with respect. We can strive to understand our peers' backgrounds or help classmates better understand our own. It's a win-win situation where involved people appreciate diversity.

On the flip side, many people find themselves in situations where their culture is either mocked or deni-

Because we live in an increasingly multicultural world, it's more important than ever to understand the pitfalls of cultural appropriation.

grated in some way. They must then decide how to deal with offenders. In turn, the offenders very often have unintentionally offended others, and they must decide whether or not—and if so, how—to make amends. Given the diversity in schools, it's essential for everybody to learn effective ways of interacting with people from other cultures.

Indeed, according to the US Department of Health and Human Services, in 2014, 54.1 percent of students ten to nineteen years old were white. With shifting population trends, that number is projected to drop to 40.3

The Native American dreamcatcher is a symbol that has been appropriated many times over. It has been commonly adapted into jewelry.

percent by 2050. Other races will also experience shifts in demographics, with some growing and others shrinking in size. No matter how these trends play out, what's certain is that every student will more regularly interact with peers of diverse racial or cultural backgrounds.

The categories of race tracked by the US Census Bureau in the 2010 US census were "White, Black or African American, American Indian and Alaska Native, Asian, and Native Hawaiian and Other Pacific Islander." In addition to the categories of race, the US Census Bureau also tracks whether or not somebody is of Hispanic origin. Beyond race, individuals may identify with a certain ethnic group. Ethnicity refers to groups with shared racial, national, linguistic, or cultural backgrounds.

Each group has its own culture and subculture which includes identifiable elements, artifacts, symbols, and other things. Clearly, those belong to the involved group. But do they own them?

The concept of ownership often comes up when addressing cultural appropriation. There are some who believe that it is impossible to assign ownership of any facet of a culture. Some even go so far as to argue that the impossibility of assigning ownership for cultural elements means that there is no such thing as cultural appropriation.

Many minorities disagree. They say that their long-time use of a particular element equals ownership. For example, large hoop earrings and certain braided hairstyles have a long association with black culture. Non-blacks adopting these styles is an example of cultural appropriation. Other examples include non-Native people wearing clothing and jewelry with designs that resemble Native American dreamcatchers, and people who are not of South Asian descent wearing bindis on their foreheads. The challenge comes in making peace about such styles, symbols, and items.

THE MAINSTREAM AND THE MELTING POT

In discussions about culture, several concepts often crop up. One is the idea of the mainstream, which means the dominant culture. In discussions about race relations, it almost always means white people. All too often, whiteness and the mainstream get set up as the standard for what is right or acceptable. Minorities are

TO TATTOO OR NOT TO TATTOO

When something from another culture becomes trendy or popular, the cultural origin can be misunderstood or completely lost. One such example is a tattoo inspired by another culture, or done in a particular cultural style.

In a January 2016 article for Everyday Feminism called "11 of the Most Culturally Appropriated South Asian Accessories—And What They Really Mean," Singaporean writer Aarti Olivia Dubey explores how tat-

The hands of the Indian bride seen here are adorned with a traditional Mehndi design.

toos of Hindu gods and henna have become popular in the Western world, even though the tradition and significance behind such body art has been lost in translation. A non-Hindu person with a Hindu god tattooed on their body might offend a Hindu person because even where the tattoo is inked on the body matters in the Hindu tradition. Regarding henna, Dubey points out that because the paste used to make designs on the skin is not permanent, it's not really a "tattoo" at all! Just as understanding of henna as a material is warped, so too is understanding of the application. Dubey explains, "It seems to have fallen into the unfortunate pit that is 'new age spiritual hipster living.'...the designs that we have been placing on our hands and feet are a symbolic representation to awakening the inner light, an ode to the sun."

cast as inferior, and their cultural items available for the picking because they are outside the mainstream.

The "melting pot" is another familiar term. This concept is intended to refer to different cultures mixing and co-existing harmoniously. Of course, harmonious race relations is an ideal that is not always achieved. The melting pot has been called into question as a goal, too. Critics point out that, in the melting pot metaphor, cultural differences disappear as a diverse society becomes more homogeneous. They say it would be better to see society as a salad bowl or mosaic, in which cultures mix but elements of them are still preserved.

Understanding that white privilege exists can help white people identify their own behavior that may show insensitivity to people of other races or cultures.

UNDERSTANDING PRIVILEGE

Within the broader discussion of race relations, the issue of privilege is often raised as well. Privilege allows people to do and say things others cannot, or it assures access to benefits other people can only dream about. One of the most widespread forms of privilege is white privilege, or the advantages that white people get simply because of their race. White privilege means that

Going to the movies can be fun, but it's important to consider how characters of different cultural or racial backgrounds are represented in a film, especially if the content seems stereotypical or negative.

Caucasians can apply to any job without fear of being shut out due to their race. It is also what allows whites to go wherever they want without fear of personal harm.

Those who do not benefit from privilege are considered the "other." The concept of "other" impacts every area of life, and is often showcased in literature and film to demonstrate the stark differences between whites and nonwhites. People who fall in the "other" category may experience prejudice in school or be bullied, and cultural appropriation is one example of such behavior.

APPROPRIATION DENIAL

Some people may feel there are still reasons to deny appropriation is an issue. Their explanations might seem like new arguments, but if we look closer, we can see how they relate to concepts we have already touched on.

For instance, some may argue that there is no such thing as appropriation because minorities themselves often adopt aspects of white culture. This brings the concept of the melting pot to mind, and we must remember why this is problematic. Minorities have a long history of being forced to adopt white language, clothing, and behavior to survive. Sometimes survival means losing a part of their cultural identity, but many families work diligently to preserve cultural elements so they can hand them down to the next generation.

Another argument would be that appropriation is really just showing appreciation of a specific culture. This argument can be an excuse for an appropriated element that has become mainstream. True appreciation entails honoring a culture and giving credit to its members for specific achievements, or celebrating it by engaging openly with people of that culture. When people adopt cultural symbols with no thought to whom they might be offending, or reduce a culture to one symbol, then they are not engaging in appreciation, but theft.

The issue is undoubtedly complex, but that doesn't mean we should dismiss it or give up trying to understand what cultural appropriation is and why it is harmful.

CHAPTER TWO

CULTURE WARS

Cultural appropriation is challenging because though it seems obvious that it can perpetuate stereotypes and reinforce false perceptions about various cultures, many people have a hard time understanding what appropriation is and what examples apply. For example, Hal Niedzviecki, a white male editor in Canada, wrote a May 2017 article in defense of cultural appropriation in literature. He suggested an "Appropriation Prize" be awarded to writers who best appropriate another culture, but many people responded online that the editor was clueless about cultural identity and that his comments were insensitive.

Another challenge is that appropriation takes many forms. So what other examples can help you identify it? In the fashion industry in the fall of 2017, famous sisters Kendall and Kylie Jenner released a handbag that looked like a Chinese food container and was imprinted with "KK Express" in a Chinese-inspired font. The bag was met with controversy, and sparked discussion of cultural appropriation.

The food industry is incredibly competitive, but stealing tortilla-making techniques, as the two Portland entrepreneurs did, is wrong.

In another instance, two white American women started a breakfast burrito business in Portland, Oregon, after vacationing in Mexico. They fell in love with the tortillas there. In an interview about the authentic taste of their fare, one of the owners explained how they learned to make them. She said while in Mexico they initially had trouble getting needed information for making tortillas. Thus, they resorted to "peeking into the windows of every kitchen." The fact did not trouble them, but outraged many readers who accused the women of cultural appropriation because of the way they gathered their information. Shortly after the interview was published in a May 2017 issue of *Willamette Week*, the women closed their business, and Huffington Post published another article about the situation that labeled the theft a form of cultural appropriation.

The burrito business is an example of how the issue plays out globally. Indeed, cultural appropriation is a worldwide problem with no culture or country spared. Individuals, businesses, and other entities all engage in activities designed to benefit themselves at the expense of other cultures.

WHY IT HAPPENS

While members of any culture can be the perpetrators of cultural appropriation, it is usually defined in terms of cultural elements being co-opted by members of a society's dominant culture. A dominant culture is boss—it has most or all of a nation's power, influence, and resources. Victims of cultural appropriation usually don't have those. They lack wide-range influence. They do not have resources or power to fight the behavior they endure. They can complain about behavior, but they can't stop it alone.

These individuals are marginalized. They are on the fringes of society in terms of power and influence. Nonetheless, they are citizens with rights. For example, American minorities have rights. But they do not have the power and influence of white citizens or big corporations. It's a fact that makes cultural appropriation such a thorny issue in the United States.

WHAT'S THE BIG DEAL?

Some people live and attend school in very diverse areas of the United States. Others attend predominantly white or black schools. Whatever their school makeup, students must understand the importance of effectively living among, and interacting with, other cultures. That is important for several reasons.

For example, your family may move to a new area. Your new neighborhood or school may be more culturally diverse than your former home was. Or you may choose to attend a college with a demographic makeup unlike that of your high school.

Maybe you opt for military service in the future. That career may take you to areas of the United States that have a greater mix of cultures, or you may serve abroad. Many military personnel work in countries among people of different cultures. They have to learn to speak the native language, at least a little. They also must quickly learn how to work effectively and respectfully with people who are not of their same culture.

Understanding what fosters cultural unity and what might trigger misunderstanding helps. Imagine someone using something of yours without permission. What do you do? The answer will probably vary greatly based on who's using your stuff.

An invited guest? No problem—you two are friends, often swapping clothing, tech toys, and more. A tourist? Irritating, but you give him a pass; he unknowingly violated your area's "house rules" and just needs some enlightening. A stealthy stranger? You feel obligated to do or say something; that person has deliberately invaded your space without warning, stealing your stuff without regard to your feelings.

These three scenarios provide a clue to the complex issue of cultural appropriation. They are loosely based

Whether you're a guest, a tourist visiting a new place, or even just learning about the customs of someone else's culture, being respectful and mindful of others is key.

on the explanation African American writer Nisi Shawl gives in her 2005 essay, "Appropriate Cultural Appropriation." Shawl describes three types of writers and audiences—"guests," "tourists," and "invaders"—who engage in cultural appropriation in literature.

There are examples of cultural appropriation in many art and media forms. Victoria's Secret was slammed for having one of its models wear a Native American headdress while modeling underwear in their 2012 fashion show. In another instance, Taylor Swift was accused of cultural appropriation for the 2017 music video

Elements of black music have been appropriated for decades. Beyoncé is one of many black singers whose work has been "borrowed" from.

of her song, "Look What You Made Me Do," which many argued borrowed from the "Formation" video in Beyoncé's *Lemonade*.

How would you feel if something important to your culture was used without your permission? Considering examples from your own life and culture can help you feel empathy for others. Empathy can be vital to understanding where someone is coming from when they identify something as appropriation of their culture.

PRIMARY CAUSES

There are many reasons that cultural appropriation happens. Common reasons include ignorance, cultural insensitivity, privilege, financial gain, and media influence.

Related to these reasons is a concept known as tone-deafness. In music, the term means a person can't distinguish between different notes. It also refers to somebody's inability to understand how the things they say may be understood and interpreted by others.

When people are tone-deaf, they can be guilty of cultural appropriation without even being aware of it. They can't imagine how people of another culture might perceive or be offended by their actions. They may make jokes that perpetuate stereotypes. They may wear a piece of clothing or jewelry with a long, complex history in another culture and act as if they just discovered it.

WHERE IT HAPPENS

Cultural appropriation happens everywhere. People can encounter it at school or on a field trip to a museum.

Public spaces like museums are great for learning about the artwork, customs, or iconography of different cultures, but even museums can be guilty of displaying work that qualifies as appropriation.

They can come across it while watching TV, movies, or videos. If someone works part-time, they can face the issue at work. People may also run into situations in any of the public spaces they visit, from grocery stores to amusement parks.

Every industry is affected—including education, fashion and beauty, the media, Hollywood, publishing,

TOO REAL TO DISPLAY?

In 2016, the white female artist Dana Schutz created a painting called *Open Casket*. It depicted the body of Emmett Till, a black boy killed by lynching in 1955 while visiting relatives in Mississippi. Photographs of Till's open coffin at his funeral shocked the nation and world, sparking an onset of activism that helped lead to major civil rights changes in the United States. Schutz's painting was based on these photographs.

Open Casket attracted protest when it was included in an exhibit at the Whitney Museum in New York City in 2017. Critics felt Schutz did not take into consideration the cultural and political implications of Till's murder and that her painting was yet another example of a white person profiting off of the suffering of African Americans. As British-born black artist Hannah Black argued in a Facebook message, "The subject matter is not Schutz's ... White free speech and white creative freedom have been founded on the constraint of others, and are not natural rights. The painting must go." The museum disagreed. What do you think?

sports, and tourism. In essence, there may be no space in which cultural appropriation does not happen in some way. As with racism, we may face the issue even in our own homes. It can be uncomfortable to notice that your family members say, own, or wear things that they don't understand the complex cultural roots of. For example, your non-black brother might use African American slang or your non-Tibetan sister might decorate her room with Tibetan prayer flags because she thinks they look cool. You may even realize you've been guilty of cultural appropriation yourself in the past. Whatever the case may be, reflecting on past incidents, whether from your own life or from history, will help you determine how to approach the discussion of cultural appropriation.

MYTHS AND FACTS

MYTH: Cultural appropriation is a recent issue and it rarely happens.

FACT: Cultural appropriation is a global issue. In the United States, it continues to be a widespread problem, affecting numerous industries and impacting many different cultures.

MYTH: All sport teams' names, mascots, and related symbols are harmless because really, it's just a game.

FACT: Some are insensitive to the cultures they depict, negatively influencing other people's image of the relevant cultures.

MYTH: If I share my concerns about cultural appropriation, other people will think I'm just overly sensitive.

FACT: Your feelings matter—if you think something is offensive, share your concerns so other people can better understand cultural appropriation, how pervasive it is, and how not to offend people from different cultural backgrounds.

CHAPTER THREE

STEEPED IN HISTORY

People have come to the United States for many reasons. Religious freedom, safe harbor away from war zones, and aspirations to become the next American rags-to-riches success story are only a few. Others simply want to live in a country where different races and cultures mingle freely. They feel that America offers more hope than their homelands, despite the nation's history of racial inequality. In truth, many people who immigrate to the United States never experience a life totally free from such challenges. Sure, many realize other dreams. But the United States, like other countries, still grapples with racism.

Cultural appropriation is a part of the history of racism on US shores. To better understand why appropriation occurs, it is important to understand how it is tied to such history. Racism even predates the earliest days of the nation, as we know from the way Christopher Columbus and his crew took over what they considered a New World. They assumed the role of the dominant culture over Native Americans, and the trouble began there.

27

Racism, cultural differences, and the inability to communicate were the first steps in damaging Native American identity. Native populations were greatly diminished due to genocide, or mass killing, at the hands of European settlers in Columbus's time and in the centuries that followed. Native Americans were driven off the lands they had long occupied, with many eventually confined to reservations. This mistreatment harmed not only the individual Native Americans who died or were displaced, but also the distinct cultural identities of each tribe. Native Americans have yet to fully recover from all of those things. They still fight stereotypes and endeavor to maintain their cultures.

KIDNAPPED AND ENSLAVED

Not long after Columbus abused Native Americans, other European settlers did the same to Africans. Kidnapped from their native lands, Africans were shipped to America under extremely inhumane conditions and forced into slavery.

Once enslaved, Africans were not allowed to maintain their original cultures. They were forced to learn English. They had to eat foreign food and wear strange clothing, and even these essentials were restricted. Millions of Africans were killed before slavery ended, and many lost the connections they had to their native cultures. Others were born into slavery, so their cultural identities grew from what could be passed down to them from older generations and from their own lives as slaves.

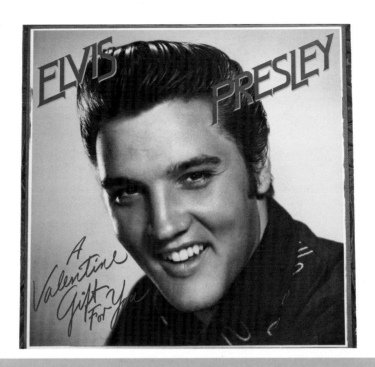

As a commercially successful white singer whose music had clear similarities to the work of black musicians in his time, Elvis Presley has become a touchstone in the discussion of cultural appropriation.

Even after slavery ended, black people were denied basic civil rights because of Jim Crow laws. Those laws assured blacks and whites would remain separate, with whites having the position of dominance. The dominant position of white culture made cultural appropriation easy. Whites took whatever they wanted from black culture. They adopted it as their own, making money off of it in many industries.

Some of the best-known cases of cultural appropriation centered on black music. White singers such as Elvis Presley copied the sounds and musical styles of

RACHEL DOLEZAL'S WHITE LIE

Rachel Dolezal's claim that she can identify as black has created controversy and further complicated the discussion of cultural appropriation.

For years, Rachel Dolezal was known as a black civil rights activist. Fair skinned, she wore her hair in cornrows and adopted other symbols of black culture. She even held a position with the National Association for the Advancement of Colored People (NAACP), a renowned civil rights organization. That changed after an interview in 2016 when a reporter asked if her parents are black.

Dolezal stumbled, admitting they are not—eventually revealing she is neither black nor biracial, but white! Her admission shocked people. Many argued that Dolezal could have successfully fought for civil rights as a white woman. Because she lied, many believed Dolezal's actions amounted to white privilege and cultural appropriation. She had adopted a nonwhite identity without being questioned and appropriated a black persona. Dolezal countered that she "identified as black." Despite her contentions, she lost much of the credibility, respect, and renown she had gained under the guise of being black.

black singers. They were able to get airplay on mainstream radio, which propelled their music to popular charts and skyrocketed record sales. Meanwhile, blacks experienced less success and made less money. Even after the civil rights movement helped abolish the Jim Crow laws, factors such as racial tension, discrimination, privilege, and differences in economic class fostered cultural disrespect that allowed appropriation to continue.

WHITEWASHING

Another example of cultural appropriation is whitewashing. Whitewashing is the tendency to cast white actors instead of people of color, extending in some cases to casting white actors to play characters who were people of color in the source material for movies. Hollywood has a long history of whitewashing. One famous example involves the first Chinese American movie star, Anna May Wong. The actress grew up in Los Angeles and broke into film in 1923, and was cast in roles that were mainly Chinese stereotypes.

Wong worked hard and received praise from critics, but even so, she was denied roles for more complex characters because she was Asian American. In Carl Van Vechten's 2003 photo series, *Extravagant Crowd*, he writes, "Later in her career, Wong was sometimes hired by studios not to play Asian roles, but to coach white actresses in an effort to help them play more believable Asian women." How insulting! The studios basically wanted Wong to make whitewashing easier for them.

Furthermore, Wong was denied the role of the Chinese main character for the movie adaptation of Pearl S. Buck's novel, *The Good Earth*. A white, German actress was cast instead, and the studio wanted Wong to play a lesser, more stereotypical role. Disgusted with the situation and with Hollywood, Wong turned down the part.

FROM THE GRAVE

Many years after Anna May Wong passed away, her image was used in an exhibit at the Metropolitan Museum of Art that seemed to bring up the question of cultural appropriation. The spring 2015 exhibit was called "China: Through the Looking Glass," and featured fashion by both non-Chinese and Chinese designers. British-Spanish designer John Galliano's dresses were inspired by the roles Anna May Wong had played, and he used Wong's image in the exhibit itself. Fashion critic Robin Givhan wrote about the exhibit for the *Washington Post* in May 2015, talking about how Wong had struggled against the stereotypical roles she was so often cast in.

Givhan writes, "There's no intent to malign those designers by suggesting they are insensitive to cultural stereotypes. The exhibition simply underscores the complicated nature of cultural representation, communication and understanding." She later adds,

"The question of cultural appropriation hums like white noise throughout the exhibition," which shows how complicated things can get when we witness something that seems like it's made to represent a particular culture.

Is there a right answer in this case? No matter what example you have questions about, it's important to keep the conversation alive and always encourage others to consider how cultural representation plays out in any form of media.

Anna May Wong made history as the first Chinese American movie star, but discrimination in Hollywood limited her success.

RACIST REPRESENTATION

When it comes to other forms of apparent representation in the United States, many schools—and a few professional sports teams— have team names or mascots that refer to Native Americans. It's a move that on the surface seems to honor Native Americans, but actually does not. In several cases, the names or mascots are obviously racist. Names that include racist epithets or mascots that are drawn in a racist, stereotypical manner fall into this group. Even names or mascots that are less evidently offensive are problematic because they reduce Native Americans to a symbol—one that is used by a dominant culture with a long history of persecuting Native Americans—instead of acknowledging them as a vibrant, contemporary cultural group. Some schools and teams have acknowledged the problem by changing their names or mascots. Others, unfortunately, have not.

Like Native Americans, Hispanics have long been forced to endure stereotypical representations of their cultures. For example, there have been many commercials for Mexican food products sold in grocery stores that feature actors with fake, exaggerated accents. These ads may also make it appear as if the idea for the food originated with white food producers. Such advertisements give viewers a one-sided view of Mexican culture and also reinforce harmful stereotypes.

IMPACT ON VICTIMS

People outside of a depicted culture often laugh at stereotypical imagery in ads, TV, and movies. For instance, an ad for salsa or guacamole might make people unfamiliar with actual Mexicans or Mexican Americans assume that all Hispanic people "talk funny" or wear particular clothing. Worse, they may erroneously believe that people from the cultures represented cannot be true Americans because they have not assimilated into mainstream America.

What is funny to those who are not affected by these mischaracterizations is gut-wrenching agony to those who are affected. These people have to constantly answer awkward questions, fight against stereotypes, or believe they must hide—rather than celebrate—their cultures.

Self-hate is one unfortunate consequence. People of color may feel ashamed of their culture, or of family members who seem similar to the stereotypical characterizations displayed in the media. To make matters worse, cultural appropriation often solidifies stereotypes, which makes it difficult to reinforce positive images of a culture that are based on truth instead of false conceptions. Even appropriation of something seemingly mundane can cause pain and be damaging to members of a particular culture.

CHAPTER FOUR

HAIR-RAISING CONUNDRUMS

Cultural appropriation shows up in areas of life great and small. It occurs even with something as seemingly ordinary as hairstyles. Those rooted in black culture have often been highlighted as particularly troublesome. The issue is decades old, but the conundrum continues to crop up.

Blacks have often complained about whites wearing hairstyles that are culturally black. They argue those individuals have no clue about the cultural importance of the styles and complain about how whites sometimes act like they invented them.

The issue occurs in many industries, including fashion, film, and music. Fashion Week is an event that showcases new clothing designs. It is a big deal, especially in New York and Paris. The designs always spark new clothing trends for the upcoming season. During the 2015 Fashion Week in Paris, two designers revealed designs inspired by Africa. Yet, all of the models were white. In addition, all of them had hair braided in cornrows, a popular hairstyle in black culture.

In another instance, in July 2017, white actress Coco Austin shared photographs of herself on Instagram. Her blond hair was braided. She called the style "Da Coco Swoop." Social media users flipped out. Many accused her of cultural appropriation. They cited various reasons for their disapproval. To them, she ignored the style's cultural history. They were upset that she had given the style a fancy name, almost as if she had created it. After all, she was mimicking a style previously worn by black female entertainers. Austin is married to Ice-T, a famous black rapper and actor. He disagreed with the criticism. He defended his wife's hairstyle, angering many people.

HYPOCRISY ON DISPLAY

Making matters worse, whites who adopt African American hairstyles sometimes get compliments for sporting looks that blacks have been criticized for or prohibited from wearing, particularly in the workplace or at school. This adds a layer of hypocrisy on top of the cultural appropriation that is taking place.

Indeed, in many workplaces, braids are not allowed. Some employers feel they do not look professional enough to wear to work. Imagine being told that your culturally styled hair is not good enough to work in!

It also happens in schools. Students are mocked for wearing braided styles. In some instances, students have been sent home. In more extreme cases, students have been expelled because of their hair! That's what

Actress and singer Amandla Stenberg has spoken out about a number of important social issues, including cultural appropriation.

happened to a seven-year-old black girl in Tulsa, Oklahoma. Although she was an "A" student, she was expelled because she had dreadlocks, another style associated with African Americans.

Some colleges have policies prohibiting "natural" hairstyles on campus. Those rules mostly apply to black people. They target those who choose not to straighten their hair with chemicals. Among other styles, natural hairdos include braids, dreadlocks, and afros.

In a 2015 YouTube video posted by *Hype Hair Magazine* called "Don't Cash Crop on My Cornrows," actress Amandla Stenberg focuses on the appropriation of black culture, including hairstyles. Stenberg provides examples and explains how appropriation separates culture from the people who originally created it. The video went viral, generating more than two million views.

DRESSED TO DISTRESS

Popular costumes for Halloween include witches, vampires, and others based on spooky themes. Superheroes are other big hits. Those outfits generally do not spark debate. However, those that allow kids and adults to dress up like someone from a different culture come under fire each year.

Popular cultural choices include stereotypical looks labeled as Native American, Japanese, and Mexican. While wearing such outfits may seem harmless, it is not. Dressing up as someone from another culture disrespects that culture's identity. It's like reducing a culture's contributions to mere outfits that can be worn for a few hours and discarded.

Think before you do it! Respect other cultures. Consider choosing something else to wear. Encourage your friends and family to follow your example. Remind them that another culture's symbols, elements, or attire is not appropriate for roleplaying, partying, or trick-or-treating.

FOOD FIGHT

In 2016, *Bon Appétit* magazine released a video that sparked debate. Many felt the video was the epitome of cultural appropriation surrounding food. The food fight was over pho, a traditional Vietnamese dish that has also become very popular among

The popularity of pho has extended beyond the borders of Vietnam, but that cannot change the dish's cultural origin.

non-Vietnamese foodies. The magazine posted about the video on Twitter. The tweet included a photo of a bowl of pho and a caption reading, "PSA: This is how you should be eating pho."

Bon Appétit was slammed because its "PSA" seemed to suggest the magazine staff knew more about a cultural dish than the very people who originated it and eat it regularly. The magazine responded positively to the criticism. They apologized, noting their cultural missteps, and took the video down.

IT'S COMPLICATED

Whether intentional or unintentional, cultural appropriation is wrong. That said, it's not always easy to tell whether or not something qualifies as appropriation. While stereotyped costumes representing other races are obviously wrong, should people be limited to only wearing costumes that represent people of their own race? Moana, the Polynesian main character in the Disney movie of the same name, has been a big hit with kids and parents. This has made Moana a popular Halloween costume choice, but some people have complained that the costume may be a form of cultural appropriation.

If you're unsure whether something is engaging with a culture or appropriating it, one of the best things you can do is ask someone from that culture how they feel about it and listen to what they have to say. You can also look for articles online that are written by people from the culture you think is being appropriated.

Even just learning more about what a dance move, piece of clothing, musical style, or turn of phrase means in the culture it comes from is helpful. If you make an art project that draws on the traditional techniques of another culture, make sure to celebrate that tradition when you present your work, highlighting your influences instead of passing off something with deep roots in another culture as you own creativity.

If you understand something in its cultural context, you are less likely to adopt it in an offensive way. Be especially alert to things that are held sacred in other cultures, and avoid treating something that others consider holy in a dismissive manner. Find out the historical reasons why certain kinds of borrowing and copying are off limits. For example, the racist history of blackface in the United States means that putting on makeup to look like someone of another race is always deeply offensive and wrong.

EAT QUESTIONS TO ASK A DRAMA HER (OR CASTING DIRECTOR)

How does the issue of cultural appropriation affect acting and theater arts differently than other industries?

What can the movie industry do to help curb complaints of cultural appropriation?

If you have ever been personally affected, how did you respond to cultural appropriation concerns?

What training do you conduct to help acting students understand and respond to cultural appropriation?

For what reasons should an actor not accept a role playing a character of a culture different from theirs?

How do you help performers authentically play roles of different cultures?

What suggestions do you have for actors about respecting the cultures of fellow performers and crew members?

How can a student positively express concerns about a school's cultural appropriation issues in its productions?

What can I do if I feel a favorite movie, TV show, or other production has culturally offensive content?

What should I do if someone accuses me of cultural appropriation because of a role I played?

CHAPTER FIVE

TEAM EFFORT

Due to its frequency and potential for major harm, cultural appropriation must be addressed whenever it rears its ugly head. People must team up.

You don't have to face cultural appropriation alone. Team up with others who are actively and courageously confronting the issue.

Everyone's help is needed! Adults, children, and teens can play a part in resisting cultural appropriation. Resistance helps spur change.

Embrace diversity. The world is diverse. That is clear from population trends in the United States and Canada, as well as in other parts of the world. You'd think that informing people of the need to embrace diversity should be a no-brainer. It's not. Racism still reigns, and cultural appropriation adds to racial strife. It makes it more difficult for people to connect

DIVERSITY IN PUBLISHING

For decades, white writers have penned stories and books about other cultures. Their books were published even as nonwhite writers were denied opportunities to share their own stories. This has been a thorny issue in the industry for decades. Efforts are underway to help nonwhite writers get published.

We Need Diverse Books is a one such development. This nonprofit organization formed in 2014 and raises awareness about the need for more nonwhite writers. It also helps provide opportunities for them. Another development is called "own voices." It is basically a push to identify writers who are penning material from their own experiences. Some topics include a writer's own culture, gender identity, and ability. Combined, these efforts provide a path for nonwhite writers to get their projects to the market more quickly and easily than in the past.

meaningfully with each other. People help resist the problem when they embrace diversity.

Stay vigilant. Be in the know about what is happening around you. Understand and avoid problematic behavior. As with other social justice issues, acknowledgment is key. You can't make a difference until you are willing to admit cultural appropriation is a problem. That may mean facing some facts you'd rather avoid. For example, some white people believe white privilege does not exist. When they are open to the possibility that it occurs, they can better pinpoint actions that harm people of color.

Face the facts. Similarly, some people believe it is impossible for nonwhites to be racist. That's

There are many ways to resist cultural appropriation, including getting involved in local activities that help you learn more about different people.

untrue! Nonwhites can engage in racist behavior. Face the fact. It is very possible that you are engaging in cultural appropriation even as you object about how others appropriate your own culture. So if someone calls you out, be open to changing your behavior.

Make amends. Were you wrong? If so, make amends. Apologize, even if an apology is not accepted or appreciated. There are times when you can't correct wrongs. For example, you can't change the fact you wore an inappropriate costume to an event. But you can avoid doing so in the future and, in apologizing, you'll display maturity and courage!

Be informed. Read articles and books about cultural appropriation. Watch videos or TV programs that offer more insight. Keep up to date on how cultural appropriation occurs in the United States and globally.

Reduce harm. Efforts to reduce harm abound. Some schools have developed student conduct policies that expressly prohibit cultural appropriation. Other schools have added instruction to help students better understand the problem. Know your school's rules and stick to them.

TIME FOR CHANGE

Activism is another way you can help address cultural appropriation. You can find plenty of online resources for organizations that are dedicated to representing particular cultures in appropriate ways. Team up with companies and nonprofit organizations that focus on

Protesting with other fans enables you to express your concern about culturally insensitive names, mascots, or symbols in sports. Protests can fight culturally insensitive issues in other arenas, too.

bringing cultures together. Volunteer or seek out part-time jobs that promote unity. Attending events that address cultural appropriation is useful, too. Schools and community organizations often sponsor these. You can also partner with your peers or families and attend events where activism is the focus. Participate in rallies, protests, and other activities.

Protesting is a great way to make your voice heard. The issue of cultural appropriation in sports has spurred some fans to rally and protest local and professional sports teams' names, mascots, or merchandise that are culturally insensitive. You can join

DIVERSITY ON THE SCREEN

The Academy Award is Hollywood's most coveted recognition of achievement in the film industry. Also known as Oscars, the awards are bestowed for, among other things, the best writing, acting, directing, and cinematography in film of the past year.

In 2015 and 2016, no minority actors were nominated to receive an Oscar for their performances in lead or supporting roles. Astonished Hollywood stars and fans used the hashtag "#OscarsSoWhite" and expressed their dismay about the lack of diversity among the nominated recipients. Stars said they would protest by not attending the event. Many TV viewers said they would not watch the telecasts of the awards ceremonies. The protests sparked renewed debate about the need for minority representation. In 2017, the hashtag trended again. More blacks were nominated. However, there remains a need for other minority groups to be represented.

those protests. Or you may voice your disapproval in other ways, such as by writing a letter to the editor of the newspaper in your school or town. Writing is powerful. Articles, blog posts, and even books have been written to fight cultural appropriation.

Posting videos like Stenberg's on social media can be an effective from of resistance, too. People can share their experiences, views, and suggested solutions, forming networks of information that help others understand the issue and promote change.

REDUCING CULTURE SHOCK

Sharing culture is another effective way of addressing cultural appropriation. Doing so can help spark
understanding of the difference between cultural
appropriation and appreciation. People can promote
understanding of their own cultures. Discussing culture one-on-one or in a small group helps debunk
myths and invites further information sharing.

Making friends with peers of different cultures
provides additional opportunities to promote understanding of your culture. Invite friends to cultural
activities. Unabashedly share cultural foods. Explain
the significance of cultural clothing, symbols, or
artifacts. Remember it's not fair to blame someone for
cultural appropriation if you're not also willing to help
them learn how to better interact with your culture.

Another option is to offer your valuable input to a
drama, music, or other school club to help them avoid
cultural appropriation. Serving as an advisor may also
provide chances for you to promote understanding of
your culture's characteristics.

Frank discussions about cultural differences have
helped companies develop more culturally sensitive
products. For example, a hijab is a head covering
worn by Muslim women. Muslim female athletes of all
ages have difficulty participating in sports where they
are not allowed to wear appropriate head coverings.
Others face challenges in wearing the hijab while participating in certain sports. In 2017, to address these

Speak out against cultural appropriation by sharing your personal experiences at school or other local public events.

concerns, some female Muslim athletes provided input to help Nike develop its "Pro Hijab." The product conforms to Muslim cultural standards, making it easier for Muslim women to participate in and enjoy their preferred sport.

BE SEEN AND HEARD

Another way you can help is by speaking out against problematic behavior. You can share your own experiences or open a dialogue with people who don't understand why certain behavior is wrong. Talk about current events, including how they affected you or your loved ones.

Know that some people may not understand why a particular situation is offensive to you. Others may not care. Despite these possibilities, don't remain quiet. Your feelings, opinions, and concerns matter. History has proven that when people speak up, issues can be addressed with positive results.

Also, speak up about cultural appropriation against others. Perhaps you are not a member of an affected culture, but you notice something awry. Share your concerns. Sometimes when one person speaks up, their friends are more apt to listen and adjust their attitudes and actions.

Finally, identify and report bullying that stems from cultural appropriation. If you or someone else is being bullied, speak up. Talk to a teacher, guidance counselor, family member, or other trusted adult. In many cases, race-related bullying can be considered a hate crime, which means there is extra protection for victims under school code of conduct policies as well as local, state, or federal laws.

FACING THE PROBLEM HEAD ON

There are many ways you can help address cultural appropriation. What works for you, however, might not be of interest to your friends. Choose to participate in ways that are most meaningful to you. Select those that let you actively join efforts to identify, address, and stop cultural appropriation.

A challenge in addressing cultural appropriation is understanding that someone else can be harmed even if you don't understand their feelings or reactions to something. Remember, it's not about you. Put your feelings aside, and consider how they feel. Be empathetic. We are living during one of the most diverse eras of all time, and engagement with others is vital.

Cultural appropriation is complex, but by working together we can promote real understanding of the issue. It's up to us to create better conditions for respectful cultural appreciation and exchange.

Finally, be proactive. Make a decision today that cultural appropriation is a real issue with real harmful effects. Choose to be part of the solution and actively engage with other cultures out of respect. Speak up about how the issue affects you or people you know.

Despite its complexity, cultural appropriation can be understood and addressed. When you better understand it, identify how it happens, and avoid taking part in it, you are better able to connect meaningfully with other cultures. That's a win-win situation for everyone.

amends Something that is done or given to make up for wronging another person, to compensate someone for a loss you are responsible for.

blackface Makeup used to darken a person's complexion to make them look like a black person; historically it is considered racist and offensive.

civil rights The rights people have because they are citizens.

conundrum An intricate or difficult problem, often used to convey how complex a problem is.

diversity To include different types of people based on one or more factors, different races or genders.

empathy The ability to be aware of, be sensitive to, or otherwise understand the feelings of another.

epithet A name, especially an insulting one.

epitome A typical or ideal example of something, whether it is a positive or negative example.

foodie A term for a person who loves food and particularly enjoys making new dishes or trying new restaurants.

genocide The mass killing of people due to racism, prejudice, or other factors.

hijab A traditional hair and neck covering worn by Muslim women, in some cases for religious reasons.

homogeneous Made up of parts that are all the same.

Jim Crow laws Laws existing from the 1890s until the 1960s that enforced separation of whites and blacks, and which led to repeated instances of cultural appropriation.

marginalized Being in an inferior position; not belonging to the dominant culture. In the US, often refers to being nonwhite.

PSA PSA stands for public service announcement, often referring to free information that will benefit the public.

tone-deafness The inability to distinguish between musical notes. In social situations, it is the inability to understand how someone may react to your actions.

tweet A social media message of no more than 280 characters and shared—or posted—on the social media platform Twitter.

viral A term associated with how quickly and widely something spreads on the Internet; often refers to videos, and social media messages.

white privilege A term denoting white people's access to benefits and privileges not afforded to other people, and solely based on their race.

whitewashing The casting of a white actor to play a character who is a person of color or the casting of white people only when there is no reason people of color could be cast as well.

FOR MORE INFORMATION

Canadian Race Relations Foundation
6 Garamond Court, Suite 225
Toronto, ON M3C 1Z5
Canada
(416) 441-1900
Website: http://www.crrf-fcrr.ca/en
Facebook: @FCRRCRRF
Twitter: @CRRF
This charitable organization was founded in 1997 and is
    dedicated to fostering racial harmony.

Historica Canada
2 Carlton Street, East Mezzanine
Toronto, ON M5B 1J3
Canada
(416) 506-1867
Website: https://www.historicacanada.ca
Facebook: @Historica.Canada
Twitter and YouTube: @HistoricaCanada
The goal of Historica Canada is to teach and celebrate
    Canadian history and citizenship.

The Hispanic Society of America
613 West 155th Street
New York, NY 10032
(212) 926-2234
Website: http://hispanicsociety.org
Facebook: @hispanicsociety

Instagram: @hispanic_society
This museum is devoted to helping advance the study of
    Hispanic arts and culture.

National Museum of African American History and Culture
1400 Constitution Ave, NW
Washington, DC 20560
(844) 750-3012
Website: https://nmaahc.si.edu
Facebook and Twitter: @NMAAHC
This museum is dedicated to sharing information about
    the history and culture of African Americans.

National Museum of the American Indian
4th Street and Independence Avenue, SW
Washington, DC 20560
(800) 242-6624
Website: http://www.nmai.si.edu
Instagram: @smithsoniannmai
Twitter and YouTube: @SmithsonianNMAI
This extensive collection covers more than 12,000 years
    of history and is one of the largest worldwide.

United States Holocaust Memorial Museum
100 Raoul Wallenberg Place, SW
Washington, DC 20024
(202) 488-0400
Website: https://www.ushmm.org
Facebook and Instagram: @holocaustmuseum
This museum is dedicated to helping visitors learn more
    about the Holocaust.

FOR FURTHER READING

Byers, Ann. *Beyond Slavery: African Americans from Emancipation to Today* (Slavery and Slave Resistance). New York, NY: Enslow Publishing, 2016.

Cunningham, Anne C., ed. *Critical Perspectives on Immigrants and Refugees* (Analyzing the Issues). New York, NY: Enslow Publishing, 2016.

Davis, Kenneth C. *In the Shadow of Liberty: The Hidden History of Slavery, Four Presidents, and Five Black Lives.* New York, NY: Henry Holt and Company, 2016.

Engle, Margarita. *Enchanted Air: Two Cultures, Two Wings: A Memoir.* New York, NY: Atheneum Books for Young Readers, 2016.

Gay, Kathlyn. *Cesar Chavez: Fighting for Migrant Farm Workers* (Rebels With a Cause). New York, NY: Enslow Publishing, 2017.

Gratz, Alan. *Refugee.* New York, NY: Scholastic Press, 2017.

Hilton, Marilyn. *Full Cicada Moon.* New York, NY: Dial Books, 2015.

Malaspina, Ann. *Nelson Mandela: Fighting to Dismantle Apartheid* (Rebels With a Cause). New York, NY: Enslow Publishing, 2017.

Mooney, Carla. *The Holocaust: Racism and Genocide in World War II* (Inquire and Investigate). White River Junction, VT: Nomad Press, 2017.

Pinkney, Andrea. *The Red Pencil.* New York, NY: Little, Brown Books for Young Readers; Reprint edition, 2015.

Turner, Pamela S. *Samurai Rising: The Epic Life of Minamoto Yoshitsune.* Watertown, MA: Charlesbridge, 2016.

Smith, Monique Gray. *Speaking Our Truth: A Journey of Reconciliation.* Custer, WA: Orca Book Publishers, 2017.

BIBLIOGRAPHY

BET (Black Entertainment Television). "Ice-T Defends Coco After the Internet Comes for Her for Wearing Cornrows." July 19, 2017. https://www.bet.com /style/2017/07/18/coco-ice-t-braids-cultural -appropriation.html.

Biakolo, Kovie. "How to Explain Cultural Appropriation to Anyone Who Just Doesn't Get It." *AlterNet*, September 22, 2016. https://www.alternet.org/culture/cultural -appropriation-pho-lionel-shriver-jamie-oliver-marc -jacobs.

Black Economic Development. "7-Year-Old 'Straight A' Black Student Expelled Because of 'Dreads'." September 04, 2013. http://www .blackeconomicdevelopment.com/7-year-old-straight -a-black-student-expelled-because-of-dreads.

Bon Appétit. "About that Pho Video." September 6, 2016, updated September 9, 2016. https://www.bonappetit .com/story/how-you-should-eating-pho.

Bradford, K. Tempest. "Commentary: Cultural Appropriation Is, In Fact, Indefensible." *NPR*, June 28, 2017. https://www.npr.org/sections/codeswitch/2017/06/28 /533818685/cultural-appropriation-is-in-fact -indefensible.

Dubey, Aarti Olivia. "11 of the Most Culturally Appropriated South Asian Accessories—And What They Really Mean." *Everyday Feminism*, January 20, 2016. https:// everydayfeminism.com/2016/01/south-asian -accessories-mean.

Education Views. "Cultural Appropriation Column Costs Magazine Editor His Job." May 12, 2017. http://www .educationviews.org/cultural-appropriation -column-costs-magazine-editor-job.

Givhan, Robin. "The fantasy of China: Why the new Met exhibition is a big, beautiful lie." *Washington Post*, May 5, 2015. https://www.washingtonpost.com/news /arts-and-entertainment/wp/2015/05/05/the-fantasy-of -china-why-the-new-met-exhibition-is-a-big-beautiful -lie/?utm_term=.933fab07e7ce.

Huffington Post. "A Portland Burrito Cart Shutters After Being Accused of Cultural Appropriation." June 1, 2017. https://www.huffingtonpost.com/entry/a -portland-burrito-cart-shutters-after-being-accused _us_59303570e4b042ffa289e7f3.

Kennedy, Randy. "White Artist's Painting of Emmett Till at Whitney Biennial Draws Protests." *New York Times*, March 21, 2017. https://www.nytimes.com/2017/03/21 /arts/design/painting-of-emmett-till-at-whitney-biennial -draws-protests.html.

Morby, Alice. "Nike Unveils Pro Hijab for female Muslim athletes." *Dezeen*, March 8, 2017. https://www.dezeen .com/2017/03/08/nike-pro-hijab-design-female -muslim-athletes-sportswear-fashion.

Opiah, Antonia. "Why The Cultural Appropriation Conversation Needs To Go Further." *Teen Vogue*, May 24, 2017. https://www.teenvogue.com/story/why-the -cultural-appropriation-conversation-needs-to-go -further.

Pauls, Karen. "'We cannot look to mainstream Canada to support us': Indigenous writers urge communities to

reclaim own voices." *CBC News*, May 16, 2017. http://
www.cbc.ca/news/canada/cultural-appropriation
-debate-indigenous-voices-1.4116615.

Peacock Thomas, and Marlene Wisuri. *To Be Free: Understanding and Eliminating Racism.* Afton, MN: Afton Historical Society Press, 2010.

Shawl, Nisi and Cynthia Ward. *Writing the Other: A Practical Approach* (Conversation Pieces). Seattle, WA: Aqueduct Press, 2005.

US Department of Health & Human Services. "The Changing Face of America's Adolescents." Accessed July 29, 2017. https://www.hhs.gov/ash/oah/facts-and-stats /changing-face-of-americas-adolescents/index.html.

Uwujaren, Jarune. "The Difference Between Cultural Exchange and Cultural Appropriation." Everyday Feminism, September 30, 2013. https://everydayfeminism .com/2013/09/cultural-exchange-and-cultural -appropriation.

Van Vechten, Carl. *Extravagant Crowd: Carl Van Vechten's Portraits of Women.* Yale University, July 28–October 18, 2003. http://brbl-archive.library.yale.edu /exhibitions/cvvpw/gallery/wong1.html.

Walker MacMurdo. "Kooks Serves Pop-Up Breakfast Burritos With Handmade Tortillas Out of a Food Cart on Cesar Chavez." *Willamette Week*, May 16, 2017. http:// www.wweek.com/uncategorized/2017/05/16/kooks -serves-pop-up-breakfast-burritos-with-handmade -tortillas-out-of-a-food-cart-on-cesar-chavez.

A

activism, 24, 46, 47
African Americans, 10, 21, 24,
   25, 37, 38
  Jim Crow laws, 29, 31
Africans, 28
  slavery, 28–29
Asian Americans, 7, 31

B

black culture, 11, 29, 30,
   36–37, 38
blackface, 7, 41

C

civil rights, 24, 29, 30
Columbus, Christopher, 27–28
cultural appropriation, 4, 6, 11,
   15, 23, 26, 29, 39, 42, 43,
   46, 49
  causes of, 22–23
  complicated, 40–41
  defense of, 17
  definition of, 4–5
  examples of, 7, 17, 21–22,
    24, 29, 30, 31, 32, 36–37,
    39–40
  harmful effects of, 16, 28, 34,
    43, 45, 51, 52

  as identity theft, 8
  many forms of, 17–18
  showing appreciation, 16
  tied to history, 27
  understanding, 6, 16
  where it happens, 23–25
  why it happens, 19, 22
  why it matters, 19–20
  why it's harmful, 16, 35
cultural identity, 16, 17
cultural insensitivity, 6, 47
cultural unity, 20–21

D

discrimination, 8, 31
diversity, 8–9, 20, 44, 45
  in publishing, 44
  on screen, 48

E

empathy, 22, 51

G

genocide, 28
global issue, 18–19

H

hairstyles, 5, 11, 36–37, 38
Halloween costumes, 4, 6, 5,

ABOUT THE AUTHOR

A former corporate publications editor and writer, Lisa A. Crayton loves writing for children and teens. She is the author or coauthor of several books for youth. She loves mentoring writers and especially enjoys speaking at writers' conferences. She earned a master of fine arts degree from National University and a bachelor's degree in public relations and journalism, cum laude, from Utica College.

PHOTO CREDITS

Cover Jon Super/Redferns/Getty Images; pp. 5, 9, 43, 52 Rawpixel .com/Shutterstock.com; pp. 7, 17, 27, 36, 43 (background) Zolotarevs/Shutterstock.com; p. 10 Wolfgang Kaehler/LightRocket /Getty Images; p. 12 Copyrights @ Arijit Mondal/Moment Open/Getty Images; p. 14 damircudic/E+/Getty Images; p. 15 John Eder/The Image Bank/Getty Images; p. 18 Joshua Resnick/Shutterstock.com; p. 21 Michaelpuche/Shutterstock.com; p. 22 Mark Davis/WireImage /Getty Images; p. 23 Takashi Images/Shutterstock.com; p. 29 Dan Kosmayer/Shutterstock.com; p. 30 Splash News/Alamy Stock Photo; p. 33 Silver Screen Collection/Moviepix/Getty Images; p. 38 Steve Granitz/WireImage/Getty Images; p. 40 Owen Franken/Photodisc /Getty Images; p. 45 Marc Romanelli/Blend Images/Getty Images; p. 47 The Washington Post/Getty Images; p. 50 Jeff Greenberg /Universal Images Group/Getty Images.

Design: Michael Moy; Layout: Ellina Litmanovich; Editor: Megan Kellerman; Photo Researcher: Karen Huang